APOSTLES OF RIGHTEOUSNESS
IN THE
MARKETPLACE

Living Right Without Losing Out

✳~~✳

OKEY ENELAMAH

APOSTLES OF RIGHTEOUSNESS IN THE MARKETPLACE

ISBN: 978-978-938-636-9
Copyright © 2014 Okey Enelamah
Produced in Nigeria

FIRST EDITION
Published by AiMP Network Limited/Guarantee
Lagos, Nigeria.

Please direct your inquiries to:
+234 803 307 2328 or +234 806 880 3956

Copyediting, proofreading and cover design by Storyteller Services

CONTENTS

DEDICATION

To my father, Reverend Fred Eze Enelamah, who entered into eternity on March 31, 1990. He laid the foundation of faith and righteousness for our family and to my mum, Mrs. Elizabeth Amukahara Enelamah who has carried on his legacy to this day.

ACKNOWLEDGMENTS

I would like to acknowledge three groups of people: the mentors who have shaped my spiritual and life journey; those who made this project possible; and my family.

I am grateful to Pastor E. A. Adeboye for his immense role in my spiritual journey; Bob Gass, for making morning devotion a delight; Dr. Okey Onuzo for his teachings on spirituality and its impact on my life; Pastor Kayode Pitan, a man of practical wisdom and insight; and lastly, but not the least, Pastor Yemi Osinbajo for his spiritual leadership and ability to articulate God's Word. I thank Mr. Richard Kramer for believing in Nigeria and believing in me. His constancy of purpose and consistency of action have helped shape who I am. I thank Dr. Christopher Kolade, a true apostle of righteousness in the marketplace, for taking the time to review the manuscript and for his willingness to write the foreword to this book.

Writing a book, I have found, is all about teamwork. I acknowledge the people who have made this book project possible. I thank my brother and friend, Udo Nwachukwu for his timely contributions. I thank our consultant, Olakunle Kasumu of Storytellers Limited, for believing we could pull it through. Many thanks to Segun Kusimo, my able Personal Assistant, who always rises to the occasion and my younger brother, Pastor John Enelamah and the AiMP team for their dedication to the project. You made it all possible.

Finally, I would like to appreciate my dearest wife, Funlola and our lovely children, Chiemela, Chisom, Chibuzo, Chizara and Munachiso. Thank you for partnering with me to build our home and letting me play my role. You make life worth living. I love you all!

Okechukwu Enyinna Enelamah
March 2014, Lagos, Nigeria

FOREWORD

Okey Enelamah opens the first chapter of this book by asking a number of questions. However, we already know, from the title and subtitle on the cover, that his objective is to show that the answers to his questions are all resoundingly affirmative. The author's purpose, therefore, is to lead us gently but firmly to the only position that he accepts – that it is possible to 'live right without losing out' by accepting the grace of God and having faith in His ability and desire to support those who choose to serve as 'apostles of righteousness in the marketplace.'

I identify fully with the author when, towards the end of the second chapter, he writes about "Combining right living and success in the marketplace", and points out that we often struggle with the subject of righteousness in that context. A few possible explanations come to mind. First, can it be that we find things difficult because our definition of 'success' in the marketplace is often flawed? The Bible tells us that we are successful when our efforts bear fruit, and Jesus Christ Himself reminds us that He wants us to bear "fruit that will last" (John 15:16). In other words, an immediate benefit may bring us only short-lived satisfaction: real success means sustainable success. We may be deceiving ourselves if we try to avoid "losing out" by abandoning the patience and consideration of other people that true righteousness demands of us. Okey Enelamah recommends that, in appropriate circumstances, we choose the option of "delayed gratification" – a word of true wisdom!

Can it also be that we sometimes forget that we are not the 'owners' of life or what we do with it, and that we are merely "stewards" of the Lord's purpose, and of the resources that He has created for the execution of His programme for the world? The word of God reminds us that one of the requirements of stewardship is that the steward should be found faithful (1 Corinthians 4:2). Since we serve a God of righteousness, faithfulness means that we should serve him by becoming 'apostles of righteousness' ourselves.

Moses charged the children of Israel to remember that the power to get wealth is given by God. We often need to remind ourselves that, in the business environment today, 'power to get wealth' comes by the grace of God; and it is frequently demonstrated through the knowledge, skills, expertise and effort that the business person must apply to the enterprise. These, too, are acquired through the generosity of our heavenly Father, and the Holy Spirit is ever present to guide us to apply them properly even when we are in doubt (Isaiah 30:21). A true apostle of righteousness in the marketplace is keenly conscious of this, and will pursue 'best practice' in the management of his business

Best practice is the only viable option for a business person who desires to represent God in the marketplace, and it manifests in a number of ways:

- The skillful manner in which we apply our God-given resources in business

- The meticulous planning of our business for true accountability

- The management of assets with a consistent sense of responsibility

- The avoidance of multiple standards in business interactions

- The avoidance of waste

- Always giving God the thanks and glory for our successes.

By writing this book, Okey Enelamah offers crucial support to all business people who feel the relentless pressure of negative trends in the marketplace and may sometimes be at a loss as to how to deal with them.   His recommendation is that we should remember that God is, in fact, the Principal Stakeholder in our business, and is keen to see that we do well by living right. After all, He made all things – including all that we use in our businesses, He has foreknowledge and He is the best authority to lead us to the place where we never lose out. What makes us so certain?   The Lord loves His people, and His resources are truly without limit. Above all, 'He has promised, and He will never fail' if we yield leadership to Him.

Among the many ideas that the author shares with us, he asks us to view "righteousness" from the platform of what God expects of us, and not from any comparison of ourselves with other people. He also urges all who desire the role of apostles in the marketplace to see themselves as 'principal champions' of the cause. Okey Enelamah's Apostles of Righteousness in the Marketplace is, without doubt, a timely and eminently significant contribution to business people who are committed to the lifelong responsibility of standing for Christ in the marketplace. It is a true blessing to all followers of Christ in every community of business people.

Christopher Kolade
March 2014

1

❀〜〜❀

THE APOSTLES OF
RIGHTEOUSNESS

Is it possible to live right without losing out? Is it
possible to be upright and succeed at the same time in
the business world? Can we be people of integrity in a
world of commerce that is full of corruption and
compromises? Can anyone succeed in the world's
compromised marketplace without being corrupt?
Can we be righteous in the marketplace? These are
very critical questions.

In 2009, God, through a dream, ministered to me a message that would have a profound effect on my life. This was just before the famed turmoil that unfolded in Nigeria's banking industry. In the dream, captains and business leaders in banking and other sectors of the economy were gathered in somebody's two-storey house and I happened to be there too. At a point in time, the host asked every guest to join him upstairs and everyone heeded to his invitation by heading up the stairs after him. When we got upstairs, I observed that it was full of skulls, bones and idols. Surprisingly, without any nudging, people started to bow down and worship those idols. I was shaken by what I saw and immediately found myself calling the name of Jesus until I woke up. The dream was as clear as reality to me and its interpretation, which was also obvious to me at the time, was this: idolatry and iniquity reigned supreme out there in the market place. People were committing all sorts of atrocities to achieve gains because either they didn't know any better or were simply too desperate to care.

After I had that dream, I was still pondering and meditating on it when the word of the Lord came to me in the beginning of 2010. God said that He was still looking for men and women that He can use to manifest His character and nature in the marketplace. I realised that it is not for lack of God's power that there is not a demonstration of His power in the marketplace. The challenge is a lack of faithful men and women who demonstrate that it is God who owns heaven and earth and gives the power to get wealth.

The essence of my message to you in this book is that righteous living can be combined with success in the marketplace and God is looking for people He can use to showcase the rewards of righteousness. I am saying that it is possible to be righteous and successful. The notion that we must compromise, lie, cheat, bend rules, yield to evil, worship idols or sell our souls to Satan before we can succeed in business, commerce and society in general is a very faulty one. The idea that if we stand for integrity, we will get bypassed for the juiciest deals and the best opportunities in the marketplace is an ungodly idea. God is still seeking for the kind of people – in the marketplace and in the nation – that He can use to display what He can do. God wants to demonstrate through His people that it is possible to live right and still be exceedingly successful – whether you are in politics, banking or any other sector of the economy. Basically, God is looking for *Apostles of Righteousness* in the marketplace - people who are committed to standing for what is right in God's sight in the face of obstacles.

Now let me explain the context in which I refer to the words 'Apostles' and 'Righteousness' so that you can properly understand the message I am trying to share with you.

APOSTLES

I am not dealing with the word 'Apostle' in the classic sense of the 5-fold ministry of Apostles, Prophets, Pastors, Teachers, and Evangelists. The word 'Apostles' as used in this book simply refers to *Principal Champions*. An Apostle is a principal champion of something - a promoter of a cause. To illustrate this, let me share with you an experience I recently had. I am a Fellow of African Leadership Initiative West Africa (ALIWA), which is part of the Aspen Global Fellowship Network, a values-based leadership fellowship committed to raising leaders that have the right values, ethics and ways of governing. In recent years, the fellowship was beginning to get weak and so a number of us who were concerned met to discuss how to bring it back to life and make sure it is actively playing its role in the country. Inevitably, the discussion turned to things like fund raising and one of the people who was present at our meeting started to cite examples of those who had been successful in fund raising. He gave examples of people who had successfully organised all kinds of dubious award ceremonies to raise money.

What caught my attention was that even though the values of those who organised the fund raising awards were warped, they succeeded at raising all the money they needed because they had the drive, vigour and zeal to push for what they wanted. They were champions of their cause. They pushed so hard that it was almost impossible for them to fail in their questionable objectives. The point is that nobody who makes such a quality commitment fails to get results whether or not he or she is serving God.

So, in the context of this book, the 'Apostle' is a *principal champion of a cause*. He is clear about his objectives. He possesses vision, vigour and zeal to the extent that it is impossible for him to fail.

RIGHTEOUSNESS

The word 'Righteousness' in this book is used mostly in the context of 'right living' and uprightness in everyday life. The usage of the word is meant to be simple and practical and not necessarily theological. It does not refer to the 'perfection' we receive by believing in Christ as our Lord and Saviour. Also, it does not imply the religious and spiritual arrogance often associated with the phrase, "self-righteousness".

It is nevertheless important to consider the word from a scriptural perspective without delving into theology, particularly with regards to what God expects of the believer in Christ. It is essential to understand this foundation, which is important in arming us with a clear conscience, faith and grace to be able to live right and overcome sin as we endeavour to operate daily as apostles of righteousness in the marketplace. I will address this in the next chapter.

For now, let me point out that the challenge today is a lack of commitment to right living, trusting God and being able to do so consistently in the face of difficult temptations and obstacles. I am not trying to advocate for being religious or legalistic but rather saying that it is possible to stand up for a cause we believe in until something positive happens. We need to begin to say to ourselves, "You know what? We have to be serious or we have to give it up!" We can't be talking about other people and saying, Well, their values are different and that is why they are getting results." Our values may be right but because of lack of effort, commitment and discipline, we are not getting the type of results we should be getting.

God is looking for people that believe in the cause of righteousness and are willing to stand up and be zealous for it. God is looking for apostles of righteousness in the marketplace - people that will do what is necessary to obtain God's promises, not people who will be lukewarm or those who will say to themselves, "Well they have taken over so what can we do?"

2

~ ~ ~

THE FOUNDATION OF RIGHTEOUSNESS

Let me share something you need to know that would help to deepen your conviction on the availability of God's grace to live righteously and succeed - especially in the marketplace.

Let us consider the scriptures that are central to this book: Isaiah 59: 1-2 and Isaiah 59: 14-21.

[1]*"Listen! The Lord's arm is not too weak to save you, nor is his ear too deaf to hear you call.*

²   *It's your sins that have cut you off from God.*

Because of your sins, he has turned away

and will not listen anymore.

¹⁴   *Our courts oppose the righteous,*

and justice is nowhere to be found.

Truth stumbles in the streets,

and honesty has been outlawed.

¹⁵   *Yes, truth is gone,*

and anyone who renounces evil is attacked.

The Lord looked and was displeased

to find there was no justice.

¹⁶   *He was amazed to see that no one intervened*

to help the oppressed.

So he himself stepped in to save them with his strong

arm,

and his justice sustained him.

¹⁷   *He put on righteousness as his body armor*

and placed the helmet of salvation on his head.

He clothed himself with a robe of vengeance
and wrapped himself in a cloak of divine passion.

¹⁸ He will repay his enemies for their evil deeds.
His fury will fall on his foes.
He will pay them back even to the ends of the earth.

¹⁹ In the west, people will respect the name of the Lord;
in the east, they will glorify him.
For he will come like a raging flood tide
driven by the breath of the Lord.

²⁰ "The Redeemer will come to Jerusalem
to buy back those in Israel
who have turned from their sins,"
says the Lord.

²¹ "And this is my covenant with them," says the Lord.
"My Spirit will not leave them, and neither will these
words I have given you. They will be on your lips and
on the lips of your children and your children's
children forever. I, the Lord, have spoken!"

The following are two key points from those passages:

1. The Lord is Still Able to Save

You have to approach the marketplace with the conviction that God has the power to save, bless, intervene and prosper.

This is important because at the heart of the issue is faith in God's capability to do something. Verses one and two make it clear that the Lord is still able to hear our prayers and save but the problem is that sin is interfering with the flow of God's blessings and His anointing. You need to know that God can bless anything you are doing in the marketplace that is according to His will. He can open doors for you and give you tremendous opportunities. He can side track your weaknesses and disadvantages and bless you despite them. However, sin is what will block God from acting on your behalf. If you constantly make the wrong choices – if you choose to steal, lie, cheat, short-change people and generally disobey God's instructions, you will inevitably hinder Him from intervening in your involvements in the marketplace. And don't forget that "...by strength shall no man prevail." Unfortunately, there are many people who are cheating and doing all sorts of things to get ahead because they believe that without doing so, they can't get ahead.

There is now no difference between the world and the church because there is an overflow of sin everywhere. God is saying, "I need people that will stand up." His empowering grace is available even today but it must be used to defeat sin because the grace that does not overcome sin is not God's – it's fake. We need to be clear about that. The person that is saying there is grace yet continues in sin is fooling himself. Grace is empowerment to overcome sin not to keep indulging in it. Grace doesn't cover sin, it empowers us to overcome it. That is the difference and we need to make that distinction and embrace this truth.

2.   *God Himself Came Down*

God looked and was so displeased that He had to come down. Christ came to defeat the works of the enemy and to stand in the gap for us. God has stepped in and now that Christ is here, we are in the dispensation of grace and as many of us as are willing to walk with God can be part of the excellent thing He wants to do. You need to understand the relevance of His coming. His coming means power for you to live right.

I believe we are in a pivotal season and a time of great expectations. *"As many as are willing will eat the good of the land."*

The Christian faith is built on a foundation of righteousness. There is ample evidence in scriptures that the foundation of the Christian faith is righteousness. In fact the entire bible is about sin and its consequences and God's desire to bring us back to Himself.

Hebrews 1:8 says,

But to the Son he says,

"Your throne, O God, endures forever and ever.
*   You rule with a scepter of justice"*

Matt 6:33 says,

Seek the Kingdom of God above all else, and live righteously,
and he will give you everything you need.

Righteousness is important to God. These days, people seem to dodge from this truth but it is one we have to accept. Righteousness is central and essential to our mission in this world as believers. Anyone who teaches anything contrary has missed it. We cannot continue to make the subject of righteousness irrelevant. We must say it as it is.

Psalm 89:14,

Righteousness and justice are the foundation of your
throne.
Unfailing love and truth walk before you as attendants.

Righteousness is the foundation of God's throne. The scepter means the emblem of ruler-ship. The scepter of his throne is righteousness.

In fact, the psalmist says in Psalm 66:18,

"If I regard iniquity in my heart,
The Lord will not hear" (NKJV)

It is an indisputable fact that God does not behold iniquity.

Grace and Effort

I know someone might be reading this and wondering if I am suggesting that we become righteous through human effort, being legalistic and by following a set of religious rules. No, that's not what I am suggesting. I am saying that God provides us with the grace to be able to make the right choices, resist temptation and live right but it is our duty to trust Him for that grace and use it to live right. His grace is available for us but we have to put in the effort to use that grace in the best possible way we can. In page 111 of his book *By Grace Alone – Finding Freedom and Purging Legalism from your Life*, Derek Prince wrote "We must make the effort to move from *imputed* righteousness (the gift we receive from God) to *imparted* righteousness (the way we live)."

We don't become righteous in the eyes of God by following a set of rules. We become righteous by His grace but it is our job to live out that righteousness in our walk in this world. I am saying that by His grace we can make the right choices; we can resist the temptations to steal, cheat and cut corners in the marketplace. We can turn down the urge to do what others are doing because we know that He is able to bless the works of our hands.

The point is this: the grace is available.

There is what I call **Paul's Success formula** in 1 Cor.15:10. Paul said,

But by the grace of God I am what I am, and His grace toward me was not in vain; but I labored more abundantly than they all, yet not I, but the grace of God which was with me (NKJV)

What was he saying? We are empowered by grace and we become successful at anything by grace but we have to put in the effort to maximize the grace that is available for us. Grace provides you with what you need to get the job done. When you stand up, God will pick you up. We have to understand that we are in the dispensation of grace and so we can ask for it all the time. Grace should never be far from our minds. That is why we share it after every prayer. I don't think many people have even paused to ask why we are always sharing the grace after prayers. We need it all the time. We can't afford to do without it and when you come to a revelation of grace, you realize you can't run your race without it. Like Paul, you want to be able to say, "I was not disobedient to the heavenly vision…" but by the grace of God, I lived a life that was pleasing unto Him. Please notice what Paul said: "I labored more abundantly" meaning that grace does not equate to laziness but hard work and commitment. Whenever, I am asked to do something, I ask God for grace because even the smallest thing can become difficult when grace is absent but when God is in it, very difficult things become deceptively easy because of His grace.

Hunger and Thirst for Righteousness

Jesus, our Lord, in the Sermon on the Mount admonished us to 'hunger and thirst for righteousness'. He said, *"...blessed are they who hunger and thirst for righteousness for they shall be filled."* He could have chosen any other illustration but He intentionally chose to use 'hunger' and 'thirst'. He basically meant that we need to hunger and thirst for righteousness. It has to be something we desire and press into. Our Lord does not make flippant comments. 'Hunger and thirst' was exactly what He meant. This speaks to the power of desire. So why don't we get on with the core issue? Why don't we focus on righteousness as our core desire and see what God will do?

Jesus Christ went further in Matt 6:33 when He said "Seek first". 'First' means top priority. One of the things the Lord told me recently is to focus on personal growth and pleasing Him. This reminds me of the story of Solomon. God told him to ask for anything and he made that incredible request which has become one of the hallmarks of the bible. He asked for an understanding heart and wisdom rather than material possessions. And God said, *"You did not even ask for the lives of your enemies. You didn't ask for riches. You didn't ask for long life. What you have asked for, you will have and the other things you didn't ask for will be added."* You're not cheating yourself when you seek first the things of God. I know what I am talking about because I speak from personal experience. If you seek God first, then other things will follow. There are some things that are fundamental and if you have them, every other thing will follow. There are prayers that answer all other prayers. In the business world, there are some things we say are *strategic*. In game theory, there is what you call a *dominant play*; it's a play that when you play well, winning is inevitable! That's what God is talking about. What if God comes to you for one thing, what would you ask Him? Why don't you seek the thing that will bring every other thing?

This is why righteousness is so fundamental. When you are in right standing with God, you position yourself to enjoy His support and blessings in your business endeavors. If you do what is right in the marketplace; if you constantly ensure that your conscience is clear and your actions align with God's word, you can experience His supernatural interventions in your affairs.

Different Levels of Commitment

I believe there are degrees and different levels of commitment to righteousness. This is why the Lord Jesus said to the Jews of His day in Matt. 5:20,

For I say to you, that unless your righteousness exceeds the righteousness of the scribes and Pharisees, you will by no means enter the kingdom of heaven. (NKJV)

He indicated the need for their righteousness to 'exceed that of the Pharisees'. So, what was wrong with the righteousness of the Pharisees at that time? It was mere religion. They were counting who came to church more, who gave more money, who had more titles and such things. There was no spirit in it, only the letter and you know, the bible says, *"The letter killeth…"* I am referring to having a deep passion for genuine righteousness. I am not referring to outward, religious, hypocritical kind of righteousness. I am talking about a pure type that flows from inside by the Holy Spirit. This requires being zealous for the things of God. It is summed up in the following passage in Philippians 2:12-13:

[12] *Dear friends, you always followed my instructions when I was with you. And now that I am away, it is even more important. Work hard to show the results of your salvation, obeying God with deep reverence and fear.* [13] *For God is working in you, giving you the desire and the power to do what pleases him.*

The Daniel Example

Dan. 1:8,

But Daniel purposed in his heart that he would not defile himself with the portion of the king's delicacies, nor with the wine which he drank; therefore he requested of the chief of the eunuchs that he might not defile himself.

This passage is not saying there was anything wrong with all the other people that were in Babylon. It was just referring to Daniel's own zeal for God and for righteousness. Daniel decided in his heart he didn't want to partake of the delicacies of the kingdom of Babylon because the foods were dedicated to idols before they were eaten. The problem was that the person who was to look after him, the Chief of Staff, was concerned that he might not look his prime and might not have the strength to carry out his daily activities and so his job would be on the line. But as Daniel began and continued the fast, he was glowing. The God of Israel became his strength. Now, that is

24

different from someone who is just going through the motions because everyone else is doing it. What we are talking about is a passion and commitment that flows from the heart. God will give us that passion in Jesus' name.

The bible says that Daniel and the three other Hebrews referred to in Daniel chapter one were ten times better than all their peers. Jim Collins in his book, Great by Choice, referred to companies that are ten times better than their peers. Daniel and his friends were found to be ten times better than their peers in ancient Babylon. Even today, there are people who are ten times better than their peers as Jim Collins points out. The question is which path are you going to take to get there?

There are many ways to get ahead in life. Some go to idols and some lean on other people or trust in their own efforts and hard work alone but when a man receives grace from heaven and at the same time works hard, it's a different ball game. Only a person, who hasn't experienced it, will doubt it.

Combining Right Living and Success in the Marketplace

I have often wondered why we struggle with the subject of righteousness. One thing we need to deal with upfront is what I call the *Either-or-Fallacy*. Most of the time, people say it is either A or B but the reality is that there are times when it is A and B, so you need to consider this possibility whenever people tell you to choose one. There was a book I read on behavioral sciences *(Predictably Irrational by Dan Ariely)* and one of the things I took away from it is that when a new product comes out, it typically sells slowly. But when they give people options, it tends to move faster. When they say that you can choose to buy any of the super, medium or the children's size, it moves faster. It is as if people feel "compelled" or drawn to make one or the other choice in those situations. It is the same thing in our lives.

It's as if we have believed in a lie that in order to succeed, we have to compromise by choosing prosperity or uprightness. They say people can't succeed in Nigeria unless they lie, cheat, compromise, give bribes and do whatever is wrong. They suggest that we must bow down to idols, compromise and suck up to human beings just because we want to get ahead. I believe there is an alternative. You can be seriously loyal to God *AND* still get ahead. You can have integrity, dignity and respect with your success. You can prosper and still hold up your head high.

Don't Just Start Well, Continue to Do Well

One of the things the Lord spoke to me about when He gave me this message the first time, is that people often don't start out bad. It is when the competition starts that they get desperate and start making wrong choices and decisions in order to stay ahead.

The bible says in Galatians 3:3,

"Are you so foolish? Having begun in the Spirit, are you now being made perfect by the flesh?" (NKJV)

You started in the Spirit by trusting God, why don't you go deeper in the Spirit by seeking Him more diligently?

My father used to say that "A little thing is a little thing but faithfulness in a little thing is a big thing." If you believe that this God is even possibly real, why don't you discover Him for yourself? Find out for yourself by discovery and experience rather than the opinions of men. Test for yourself. Find out by empirical evidence, the reality of the truth. What we are talking about is a person deciding and saying to himself, "I'm going to follow God and get to know Him for myself. If I find out it's not working, I will leave but I'm not going to be lukewarm. I'm not going to be one leg in, one leg out." I am talking about apostles of righteousness — people who are champions for God and who are prepared to stand up for what is right and who are convinced that with commitment, they will get the right kind of results. I believe that God is looking for such people today.

3

❦ ⁓ ⁓ ❦

DELAYED
GRATIFICATION

One of the reasons people struggle today is because they fail to delay gratification. In other words, they can't deal with the gap between when the price is paid and the reward comes. This is a major reason for moral and ethical failings in the marketplace. You cannot be an apostle of righteousness in the marketplace unless you have learned the value of delaying gratification.

Patience is delayed gratification. Psychologists, sociologists and scientists have found out that people who are prepared to delay gratification, go further in life. You may know about the *Stanford Marshmallow Experiment* that was done in California way back in the 60's and early 70's with children that were given candies. The children were told that those that were prepared to wait will get two candies while those who were not prepared to wait would get one candy each. The ones that were prepared to wait, according to that study, went on to do much better in life. It's the same challenge we're facing today. If you are prepared to make the sacrifice, you will get the results. But there is a price to pay and I believe it's a price worth paying. Why do we want to keep circling the mountain when we can move into the Promised Land? Like God said to the Israelites, *"You have circled this mountain long enough, now turn north"* Turn north means to face God and His promises squarely.

Let me share a personal testimony that will illustrate delayed gratification. I was once involved in a property development project and at a stage, it looked like things were very rosy and we thought we couldn't be luckier. Property prices were going up and so we believed that before we finished the development, people would come and pay up. But unfortunately, as we finished the development, the property market went down. Initially, we thought it was going to be a short-term thing and we would soon get people to buy or rent our new property and so we decided to wait. We waited for two years and then, eventually, one of the multinationals came and said they liked it and wanted all six apartments. They were going to pay us multiple years of rent and the proposal looked very attractive. We had started to thank God, believing that it was a done deal, when the test came. I was overseas when I got a call. I thought the call was to clarify one or two minor issues but unfortunately it was the broker of the transaction who was on the phone and his news was not good. He said that they had squeezed the commission so much that they could no longer afford to settle the accountant and others who would process the payment and so I had to bring two and a half percent of the proceeds I was to collect to "settle" the accountants. When I refused that request, the transaction was blocked. That is how determined people can be in the marketplace. They will even go as far as framing you to get ahead. In that particular transaction, at some stage, they wrote a dubious letter on our behalf saying we were no longer interested in the deal.

We live in a world that is compromised but God is looking for people He can work with. We had to wait for more than a year to get a deal done on the property. Eventually, God sent us help. We got the right tenant who turned out to be like "...*the blessing of the Lord that maketh rich and addeth no sorrow...*" We have had peace and at the end, everything went well but we had to be patient and we had to pass that test. If we hadn't passed that test, the entire project would have brought a lot of 'sorrow' for a long time.

It is very important that you choose the side you belong to and stick to it. When you are consistent, God will show up but you will be tested and the results will come only when you pass the test.

Let me tell you a story that is even more compelling. It is about Pastor E.A Adeboye, the General Overseer of the Redeemed Christian Church of God. He said that when they were building the famous camp ground along Lagos- Ibadan express road, South West of Nigeria, there was a particular culvert they had to build. They assumed that since it was within the camp, they had jurisdiction over it. But one day, people from the Ministry of Works came with papers and said that anything that had to do with culverts was under their ministry even if it was just to cross from the prayer room to the office, hence they needed the ministry's approval for it. Eventually, the ministry officials said, "We can sort this matter out for you if you pay us a particular unofficial amount otherwise, the ministry might have to bring down the culvert." This was a problem because they had already built the culvert to a reasonable extent.

So Pastor Adeboye said, "Listen, we are trying to build a holy camp ground for which we believe we've been given a godly vision. If I start paying you bribes now not to bring down the culvert, when am I going to stop?" That didn't satisfy them, so they brought in their bulldozers and tried to uproot the culvert. Amazingly, they tried all they could but the culvert didn't lift. It was a miracle! That was one of the many tests they had to pass. It will always be the same with everyone. Your character, integrity and resolve will be tested. You can rationalize doing wrong in many ways and say, "Well, this thing is for God. I'm going to give it to the church, the church needs it anyway" but God doesn't need that kind of help!

The Link between Faith and Righteousness

When you rationalize sin, you limit God and that

simply means, lack of faith. This takes me to the link between faith and righteousness. Genuine faith and righteousness go hand in hand.

The bible says in Hebrews 11:6 (NKJV):

⁶ But without faith it is impossible to please Him, for he who comes to God must believe that He is, and that He is a rewarder of those who diligently seek Him.

In other words, to please God, we have to exercise faith and we have to do it with diligence because He says He rewards those who diligently seek Him. That word, *diligence* has to do with discipline and perseverance. It's not a lukewarm word. The bible has several examples of people who attained that level of commitment, diligence and zeal for righteousness. One example is Abraham. The bible says in Romans 4: 20-22:

²⁰ Abraham never wavered in believing God's promise. In fact, his faith grew stronger, and in this he brought glory to

God. [21] He was fully convinced that God is able to do whatever he promises. [22] And because of Abraham's faith, God counted him as righteous.

In other words, your faith will be tested and when you pass the test, you will be counted as righteous. The grace to exercise that kind of faith exists and is available but one has to desire and draw it.

In the book of James, talking about the link between faith and righteous living, the bible says in James 2: 18-24:

[18] Now someone may argue, "Some people have faith; others have good deeds." But I say, "How can you show me your faith if you don't have good deeds? I will show you my faith by my good deeds."

[19] You say you have faith, for you believe that there is one God. Good for you! Even the demons believe this, and they tremble in terror. [20] How foolish! Can't you see that faith without good deeds is useless?

[21] *Don't you remember that our ancestor Abraham was shown to be right with God by his actions when he offered his son Isaac on the altar?* [22] *You see, his faith and his actions worked together. His actions made his faith complete.* [23] *And so it happened just as the Scriptures say: "Abraham believed God, and God counted him as righteous because of his faith." He was even called the friend of God.* [24] *So you see, we are shown to be right with God by what we do, not by faith alone.*

Abraham obeyed the command he was given because he was sure that he heard God. In other words, faith and works go hand-in-hand. Let me try and explain this. The thing about genuine faith is that it produces works. The fruit of faith is works. A faith that has no works is dead. It's like a dead plant. The argument about works that we can't do enough works to save ourselves is true. We can't work enough to earn our salvation. But having received that faith, it has to produce works. As you live by that faith, the works will show. You will be a changed person. The bible says in 2 Cor.5:17 that we become a new creation in

Christ Jesus.

Understanding faith, which is basically trusting in God for the final outcome, and righteousness, which has to be demonstrated in hard work and discipline, provides a strong basis for being able to delay gratification. Once you are able to delay gratification, you can overcome many temptations in the marketplace that are guaranteed to give you short-term benefits for long-term pains. Delayed gratification is critical for succeeding as an apostle of righteousness in the marketplace.

4

❈〜 〜❈

EXAMPLES OF APOSTLES OF RIGHTEOUSNESS

Let's look at some examples of apostles of righteousness. The bible provides many examples we can emulate. This generation is called to do what those before us have done, so there is nothing that we have been called to do that is new. Men have lived out this faith and have benefited from it and we are being called to do likewise.

ABRAHAM

Let me remind us of a story that happened between *Abraham* and Lot, his nephew in Genesis 13. Abraham had a problem with Lot and it was already leading to a major strife between their herdsmen. Because Abraham wanted to avoid striving, he said, *"You choose one way and I will go the other way"*. The interesting thing is that if you look at it in the light of 1 Corinthians 13, the God-kind of love, you will notice that love is patient and kind. It is not jealous, it is not boastful, it is not proud and it does not strive. But what enables one to exercise that kind of love? I believe it is faith in God — it is being an apostle of righteousness. When you know it is God that elevates a man, like Abraham, you will be confident about your future prospects, knowing it is not in the hands of men or achieved through striving with men. People, who have faith, understand this and look up to God. Their faith response is "How do I please God?" The bible says, *"The battle is not to the strong, nor the race to the swift… but time and chance happens to them all."* Time and chance relates to the God part of the equation. God is a major factor in human affairs. There is a God that rules in the affairs of men and it is extremely wise to seek to please Him. That is what Abraham did.

NOAH

What about *Noah*? Noah's obedience in respect of righteousness is a very important lesson for all of us. In Heb. 11:7, the bible says,

[7] By faith Noah, being divinely warned of things not yet seen, moved with godly fear, prepared an ark for the saving of his household, by which he condemned the world and became heir of the righteousness which is according to faith. (NKJV)

What is the bible saying? The bible is saying be careful you don't join those who are saying it is impossible to live righteously in Nigeria today. Like Noah, you need to live your life in a way that will demonstrate God's faithfulness and the rewards of righteous living. To the man who says it is impossible to live righteously, it is self-fulfilling because he has no faith for it, and to the man who says it is possible, he is also right because his faith will empower him to do so. Every story has two sides. The man who lacks belief "knows" what he is talking about; he knows that he can't do it. As for you who knows that God is real and rules in the affairs of men, just live it out and you will see the rewards. The bible says that Noah condemned the world when God poured down the flood. It was too late for them then. I pray that it will not be too late for you in Jesus' mighty name.

DANIEL

What about *Daniel*? He purposed in his heart that he will not defile himself with the portion of the king's

44

meat, wine and delicacies. And like I said before, he came out much better than his peers and this shows that it is possible to trust God and obtain a better result that accords with His will. That really is the heart of my message. In other words, by being an apostle of righteousness, you are showing that it is possible to be righteous AND successful at the same time. Living righteously never means that you are giving up. It means you are using a superior method that you believe in. If you believe in God, then believe in Him wholeheartedly. If you want to trust God, then trust Him totally. If you want to walk with God, then walk with Him all the way. Don't mix things up. You cannot believe in God and be lukewarm at the same time. Be zealous for Him and God will demonstrate His power through you in Jesus' mighty name. This is the primary lesson we learn from Daniel's three associates, Shadrach, Meshach, and Abed-nego.

In Daniel 3: 16 – 18 we read:

¹⁶ Shadrach, Meshach, and Abednego replied, "O Nebuchadnezzar, we do not need to defend ourselves before you. ¹⁷ If we are thrown into the blazing furnace, the God whom we serve is able to save us. He will rescue us from your power, Your Majesty. ¹⁸ But even if he doesn't, we want to make it clear to you, Your Majesty, that we will never serve your gods or worship the gold statue you have set up."

This is the kind of conviction and commitment God is demanding from apostles of righteousness in the marketplace.

DAVID

What of *David*? He was a very successful king and soldier. But he was also the psalmist and worshipper that we all talk about. He was zealous for God. In other words, David combined his love for God with real success in the marketplace. He was very good at what he was called to do either as a king or soldier. But even in doing that, he had a love affair with God that was exemplary and we still talk about David and his heart of worship till today. That is why the bible says in 1 Sam.13:14,

[14] But now your kingdom must end, for the Lord has sought out a man after his own heart. The Lord has already appointed him to be the leader of his people, because you have not kept the Lord's command.

In other words, God looked for another person to take the place of Saul who was lukewarm. God is looking for champions who will stand for Him in the marketplace and in the affairs and issues of life. People that will say, *"It doesn't matter the challenge that I face, I will draw grace from God"* That grace is the only thing that is sufficient for us. That challenge you are facing is God's opportunity to demonstrate His power!

JOB

What of the example of *Job*? Job was a great man. The bible says he was the greatest of the people of the east at the time but he was a man that was blameless as well.

Job 1:1-3 says,

¹ There once was a man named Job who lived in the land of Uz. He was blameless — a man of complete integrity. He feared God and stayed away from evil. ² He had seven sons and three daughters. ³ He owned 7,000 sheep, 3,000 camels, 500 teams of oxen, and 500 female donkeys. He also had many servants. He was, in fact, the richest person in that entire area.

Then in verse 8,

⁸ Then the Lord asked Satan, "Have you noticed my servant Job? He is the finest man in all the earth. He is blameless — a man of complete integrity. He fears God and stays away from evil."

God wants to boast about you. The bible says, *"What is man that thou art mindful of him?"* Do not believe in the lie that God is not watching and He doesn't care. He cares a lot and He is interested in you. Can you live the kind of life that will make God boast about you? When Elijah said he was the only faithful one left, God told him there are still 7,000 that had not bowed down to Baal. So God keeps records. He keeps the numbers. He knows those who are His and those who are not.

PAUL

The last example I will give from the scriptures is *Paul*. Paul taught the people of his day that genuine Christianity is about modeling Christ. He said in 1 Cor. 11:1 :

"Imitate me, just as I also imitate Christ" (NKJV)

He said, *"Follow me as I follow Christ"* Can you say to

people, to your friends and those you meet along your way, "Follow me as I follow Christ?"

When I was in business school, I met a Canadian gentleman who attended an orthodox church. He said to me that in every situation, I would ask myself: what would Jesus do? How many people think that way? Pausing to ask that question gives honor to God. Make up your mind that every time something happens, you will pause to ask, "What would Jesus do?" The fact that you stop to honor His name is a big deal with God, trust me. Learn to always stop and ask the Holy Spirit before every decision. Turn that into a lifestyle and you will realize just how much difference God will make in your life!

Apostles of Righteousness in the Marketplace

Throughout history, we have had people who feared God and who proclaimed God in the marketplace and were righteous and zealous for Him. I found out that *Will Keith Kellogg*, the man who brought us

50

Cornflakes, was a godly man who stood up for God throughout his lifetime. God gave him the inspiration to make cornflakes. The same goes for **Henry Parsons Crowell**, the man who started Quaker Oats Company. He was also a godly man. **John Davidson Rockefeller**, the man who even though he was despised by people of his day, was convinced that God gave him the power and opportunity to get wealth. He focused on what God told him to do and you can see the legacy he left behind. He was among the people who established philanthropy in America by choosing to honor God and serve man with the wealth he had – in other words, he served God by serving man. These early philanthropists did things that I'm sure pleased heaven. In asset management, there was a man called John Marks **Templeton** – *founder of the Templeton* Funds. He was an apostle in the marketplace who stood up for God. He believed in doing what was right and lived his life based on that belief. He started buying stocks during World War II when everything was down but he had enough faith and became a billionaire in the next ten to twenty years.

Hal Taussig, the man who founded the travel agency called Untours, was famous for keeping none of the profits from Untours for himself. He said that the more he read his bible, the more he realized that God didn't have any desire for him to hoard all the money for himself. You have also heard of *Mary Kay Ash*, the founder of Mary Kay Cosmetics, whose popular quote: "My priorities have always been God first, family second, career third" continues to inspire numerous people in business. *The Barclay family* who started Barclay's bank is another example.

I can go on and on but the point is that God is challenging us in this hour. He wants to do great things but He is looking for men and women with zeal and commitment that will stand up for Him. David said, *"I will not give God what will not cost me something"*. Let your commitment cost you. Pay the price. It may pain you in the short term but like they say, it's not over until it is over. You will laugh last if you walk with God.

Let me remind you that there are many covenant blessings for the righteous which are of course, only obtainable through faith. In Psalm 37:1-2, the bible says,

1 *Do not fret because of evildoers,*
  Nor be envious of the workers of iniquity.
2 *For they shall soon be cut down like the grass,*
  And wither as the green herb.

NKJV

If you jump to verse 25, it goes on to say,

25 *I have been young, and now am old;*
   Yet I have not seen the righteous forsaken,
   Nor his descendants begging bread.

NKJV

Do you know a person can believe in this scripture and

obtain a reward? What did David mean by these words? He meant that those who trust in God will never suffer hunger. I believe that a lot of our faith has to pass a certain threshold to obtain the promises of God. There are many people whose faith is neither here nor there. We are talking about people who will press in until something comes out. It doesn't matter what the issue is, a solution will come out by reason of the level of engagement and commitment. A person can decide not to suffer hunger. It only takes determination, zeal and faith in God.

A Thought on How You Can Be an Apostle of Righteousness

There is a principle that cuts across all manner of prayers and it works here too. It is the *ASK principle*.

The first letter in the *ASK* principle is 'A' and it stands for *ASK*. If you ask and hunger for righteousness, you

EXAMPLES OF APOSTLES OF RIGHTEOUSNESS

will receive it. Tell the Lord you can't help yourself. Ask Him for His enablement. If you pray and ask God, He will help you.

The bible talks about those who loved righteousness and hated iniquity in Heb.1: 9. You can prioritize righteousness today as part of your prayer and supplication. The key is to desire and ask for righteousness and God will answer you.

'S' is the second letter in the *ASK* principle and it stands for *SEEK*. You can seek righteousness. The Bible says in Matthew 6:33. *Seek first the kingdom of God and His righteousness.* Will you seek God and His righteousness first and let other things follow? Will you make God and His righteousness your number one priority? Will you seek God like never before?

The third letter 'K' in the *ASK* principle stands for *KNOCK*. You knock for righteousness by deciding in your heart to KEEP THE COMPANY OF THE

RIGHTEOUS.

Psalm 1:1 says,

> [1] *Blessed is the man Who walks not*
> *in the counsel of the ungodly,*
> *Nor stands in the path of sinners,*
> *Nor sits in the seat of the scornful.*

The company we keep influences us immensely. There is no use keeping the company of the wrong people and expecting to get the right results.

I want to end where I started. Remember, it's all about His grace. Grace is about becoming and it is worked out in righteous living. It is about empowerment. It is very important that we take to heart that God's grace is always sufficient.